CAN SCHOOL IMPROVEMENT
OVERCOME THE EFFECTS OF
DISADVANTAGE?

PERSPECTIVES ON EDUCATION POLICY

Institute of Education
UNIVERSITY OF LONDON

Can school improvement overcome the effects of disadvantage?
Revised edition

**PETER MORTIMORE AND
GEOFF WHITTY**

© Institute of Education University of London 2000

First published in 1997
Revised edition 2000

Institute of Education University of London,
20 Bedford Way, London WC1H 0AL
Tel: 020 7612 6000 Fax: 020 7612 6126
www.ioe.ac.uk

Pursuing Excellence in Education

British Library Cataloguing in Publication Data:
a catalogue record for this publication is available
from the British Library

ISBN 0 85473 625 5
Produced in Great Britain by
Reprographic Services
Institute of Education University of London

Printed by Formara Limited
16 The Candlemakers, Temple Farm Industrial
Estate, Southend on Sea, Essex SS2 5RX

I1/0009-PEP No9-05-2000 (JR)

CONTENTS

FOREWORD

This book examines the powerful evidence base concerning the important impact of social disadvantage on children's educational attainments and subsequent life chances. This evidence was downplayed during the 1980s and mid 1990s under successive Conservative governments, which stressed the marketisation of education as a means of raising standards. Current policy interest in combating social exclusion provides the opportunity for a change of emphasis. Recent initiatives suggest a greater understanding by policy makers of the need to recognise the strength of links between intake and schools' results (for example through the contextualisation of such results in the new Autumn Package sent to all schools from 1998). Nonetheless, the emphasis on raw league tables remains and this continues to exert pressure on schools in challenging circumstances serving the most disadvantaged communities. The stress on raw league tables ignores the impact of school and neighbourhood context, particularly the concentration of disadvantaged students, which research has shown has a strong correlation with schools' examination and test results.

Mortimore and Whitty provide a thorough and thought-provoking overview of the impact of social disadvantage, bringing together the perspectives of educational sociology and policy analysis and the school effectiveness research tradition. The authors argue that an effective strategy for combating disadvantage requires change in educational practice, building on the school improvement tradition, and also in terms of broader educational and social policy developments. They conclude that the tendency to blame schools for the problems of society is unfair and unproductive and they draw attention to alternative strategies to support and promote the achievement of pupils with disadvantaged backgrounds.

Mortimore and Whitty's analysis does not attempt to offer simple solutions to complex problems. It makes an important contribution to current policy debate through its emphasis on both the possibilities and the limitations of using schools as levers to combat disadvantage and social exclusion.

PAM SAMMONS
Professor of Education, Institute of Education

1
Introduction

Despite the Thatcher and Major governments' refusal to acknowledge the importance of the relationship between social disadvantage and educational achievement, stark differences in the lives of pupils with different family backgrounds have not gone away, nor has the problem of knowing how best to deal with them. According to some commentators, this topic has been 'almost a taboo subject in public policy debate in recent years' (Smith and Noble 1995: 133). Teachers who have dared to mention the subject have been branded defeatist or patronising for even considering that social background can make a difference. Although some members of the Blair government have shown an alarming tendency to perpetuate such attitudes, the change of government could provide an opportunity to re-open this important public policy debate.

In schools – especially in those with high proportions of disadvantaged pupils – the issue is of crucial importance although many of us, including teachers and governors, are unclear about the best approach to adopt. If the problem in the past has been low expectations, should we now ignore disadvantage, in the hope that pupils themselves will find the necessary strengths to overcome their problems? Should we rely on adopting, and trying to instil, high expectations for pupils' achievement or are such 'hands off' approaches doomed to failure – no matter how genuinely they are intended to help disadvantaged pupils?

The lessons of history are not hopeful. Whilst some outstanding individuals have achieved the highest levels despite (or, in some cases, motivated by) their inauspicious home backgrounds, most formal education systems have failed pupils whose families are disadvantaged (Douglas, 1964; Davie et al., 1972; Essen and Wedge, 1982; Gorman and Fernandes, 1992; Mortimore and Mortimore, 1986; Osborne and Milbank, 1987; OECD, 1995). Paradoxically, those who have had most to gain from education have often been the least able to do so.

In recent years the problem has been exacerbated by the introduction of a requirement to publish examination and test results, which have been turned, by the press, into crude league tables. Parents have been encouraged to use these results to judge the quality of schools, despite the absence of any relevant information about the background or prior achievement of pupils as they enter the schools. It is thus in schools' interests to avoid admitting disadvantaged pupils who – in the absence of extra resources – would be likely to perform poorly and thus worsen the position of the school in the league tables. Such 'hard to teach' pupils are often only welcome in schools which are under-subscribed and which are desperate for extra pupils to increase their financial viability. Unfortunately, many such schools are already coping with problems to do with the low morale of staff and pupils and are not – other than in exceptional cases – in a strong position to 'lift' the achievement of disadvantaged pupils.

Meanwhile, our society appears to be deeply confused about the relationship of disadvantage to patterns of achievement. In particular, there is confusion over how much underachievement is due to the actions of individuals and how much to the influence of the school or the attitudes of the wider society. In this book, we will try to clarify some of the issues by exploring what we do know about disadvantage and the impact it can have on the life of school pupils. We will also evaluate some of the remedies that have been adopted in attempts to try to change patterns of disadvantage. Finally we will outline other approaches that appear *prima facie* to offer hope for this group of pupils and discuss both their advantages and their limitations.

2
Social disadvantage

More than fifteen years ago Mortimore and Blackstone (1982) commented that 'The concept of social disadvantage is not easy to define partly because it is a relative concept, tied to the social context of time and place' (1982: 3). Townsend (1996) sees poverty in the same relative way, as 'the absence or inadequacy of those diets, amenities, standards, services and activities which are common or customary in society'. In an attempt to provide objective measures, studies carried out by the National Children's Bureau on the effects of disadvantage adopted three 'hard' criteria: membership of a large or a single-parent family; being in receipt of a low family income; and living in poor quality housing (Essen and Wedge, 1982). The Organization for Economic Cooperation and Development draws attention not only to the multiplicative effects of such factors (with one form of disadvantage often leading to the experience of other forms) but also to the fact that much of the impact is felt disproportionately by women (OECD, 1995).

A graphic account of what being poor is actually like has been reported by Oppenheim (1993): 'Poverty means going short materially, socially and emotionally. It means spending less on food, on heating and on clothing.... Poverty means staying at home, often being bored, not seeing friends ... not being able to take the children out for a treat or a holiday' (1993: 4).

Despite the general improvement over recent years in most people's living standards, conditions have worsened for a significant minority. According to Walker and Walker (1997) the number of people living in poverty (50 per cent of average national earnings or less) has shown a threefold increase since 1979 and now stands at one-quarter of the population. The United Kingdom has been exceptional in that the difference between the 'haves' and the 'have nots' seems to have resulted from official policies designed to lift the constraints affecting the rich. These policies have also sought to penalise the poor in the interests of freeing them from a so-called 'dependency culture'. 'Britain stands out internationally in having experienced the largest percentage increase in income inequality between 1967 and 1992' (Dennehy et al., 1997: 280).

The proportion of children living in poor households is now 32 per cent, compared to the European Union average of 20 per cent (Eurostat, 1997). Researchers from the Thomas Coram Research Unit estimate that about one-third of children now live in households with no full-time earner (Brannen et al., 1997). For many such children, life is grim:

> Children from poor homes have lower life expectancy and are more likely to die in infancy or childhood; they have a greater likelihood of

poor health ... a greater risk of unemployment, a higher probability of involvement in crime and enduring homelessness. (Holtermann, 1997: 26)

WHAT IMPACT DOES SOCIAL DISADVANTAGE HAVE ON CHILDREN'S EDUCATIONAL OPPORTUNITIES?

Almost by definition, children from disadvantaged backgrounds are more likely than other children to live in a worse environment. Of course disadvantage exists in rural areas, as it does in estates on the fringes of many of our cities, but it is often in the inner city that the worst problems are found in Britain. High-density living is not, in itself, a bad thing – many people choose to live in this way – but it tends to mean living in greater proximity to crime and drugs and it frequently means living in poor quality housing. As noted by Holtermann (1997) social disadvantage is also frequently associated with poorer health. Children tend to be physically weaker and have less energy for learning than their peers. They are also more likely to be emotionally upset by the tensions in their lives. Finally, they are less likely to have the opportunity for study and for educational help at home. These are just the conditions in which children will be vulnerable to low levels of self-efficacy: 'an inability to exert influence over things that adversely affect one's life, which breeds apprehension, apathy, or despair' (Bandura, 1995: 1). They, in turn, will work against children's development as effective school learners and, ultimately, according to Wilkinson (1997) their chance of a long healthy life.

Whether the impact of disadvantage on a particular child's education is lasting or not will depend on their own resilience as well as on how much their parents are able to shield them from the effects of disadvantaging circumstances. We know from studies of educational priority programmes that the effects of disadvantage are cumulative. Each new factor adds to the problem. This became starkly evident in a recent study of the educational consequences of homelessness with which one of us was involved (Power, Whitty and Youdell, 1995).

REMEDIES ALREADY TRIED

There have been a number of distinct approaches to the amelioration of the effects of poverty on educational opportunities. We will focus, for the time being, on education-centred measures, although we shall point later to the limitations of these. One approach rests on the concept of meritocracy. First taken seriously with the introduction of public examinations for officials in the mid-nineteenth century, the concept has subsequently underpinned the widely held assumption that those with talents would rise to the top through public competition. It was used to justify the scholarship ladder introduced at the turn of the century, formed the basis of the 11-plus selection procedure and, most recently, the assisted places scheme. It has also informed the thinking behind public examinations generally. The evidence from studies of social mobility shows that such a meritocratic approach does help overcome the effects of disadvantage by promoting some individuals with outstanding talents. What such studies also show, however, is that, although this works for some, it fails to do so for many more (Brown et al., 1997). The philosophy of 'plucking embers from the ashes' of inner city deprivation (cited in Edwards, Fitz and Whitty, 1989) does nothing to improve the standard of education for those left behind. The Conservative governments introduced choice and competition strategies with an avowed aim of equalising opportunities for all families regardless of where they lived. Too often, however, these strategies seem only to have polarised provision even further (Whitty, Power and Halpin, 1998).

The second approach has been characterised by the use of compensatory mechanisms. These include individual benefits, such as free school meals, uniform grants and other special measures for low-income families. The problems with individual benefits are that the levels of funding have always been relatively modest and have thus been unable to compensate for the major differences in the conditions of children's lives (Smith and Noble, 1995). Compensatory mechanisms have also included the allocation of additional resources to schools, such as in the Educational Priority Area programmes of the 1960s and 1970s, when extra payments were made to schools with high proportions of disadvantaged pupils (Halsey, 1972; Smith, 1987). One drawback of school-wide schemes is that targeting is necessarily inefficient: some advantaged pupils will gain access to extra resources within the chosen schools, whilst many disadvantaged pupils, in other schools, will fail to do so (Acland, 1973; Plewis, 1997). However, there may still be cost-effective benefits, as work concerned with the development of 'at risk' registers of birth disorders, carried out over 20 years ago, shows (Alberman and Goldstein, 1970). Later versions of this idea, adopted by the (former) Inner London Education Authority, provided extra resources on a sliding scale rather than on an all-or-nothing basis (Sammons et al., 1983). The local management formulae for schools approved by governments over the last few years, however, allow little scope for radical positive discrimination.

The third approach to combating disadvantage involves the creation of intervention projects, potentially open to all pupils, but which have mainly been used with the disadvantaged with a view to accelerating their educational development. Such projects include: in the United States, the High/Scope programme, which promoted active child learning (Weikart, 1972; Schweinhart and Weikart 1997); the Comer Approach, which addresses children's health and social as well as educational needs (Comer, 1980); and Success for All (Slavin et al., 1993) – seen as one of the most promising approaches to overcoming the educational effects of disadvantage (Herman and Stringfield, 1995). In New Zealand, Clay has developed the Reading Recovery Programme, a structured approach to overcoming early reading failure which has been shown to be effective for disadvantaged pupils (Clay, 1982; Rowe, 1995). In Latin America there have been a number of initiatives based on the work of the late Paulo Freire. There has also been an interest in capitalizing on research which demonstrates that intellectual tasks can be found in the everyday activities of disadvantaged children (see, for instance, Nunes, Schliemann and Carraher, 1993). In the United Kingdom, the Early Years Nursery Study, which focused on ways of increasing children's capacity to learn (Athey, 1990) has also claimed some success; a series of British parent involvement schemes designed to encourage children and parents to read together (see, for example, Tizard, Schofield and Hewison, 1982) has been shown to have positive effects; and a Scottish project on the use of homework has demonstrated gains in disadvantaged areas (MacBeath and Turner, 1990).

Despite the enthusiastic support of teachers and local authorities in the UK for each of these projects, official support and hence widespread implementation has been strictly limited. The Reading Recovery Programme, for instance, was trialed in an English LEA and introduced more widely in a highly systematic way. It had £14 million spent on it through government grants and obtained positive evaluations from a carefully controlled experiment (Sylva and Hurry, 1995; Hobsbaum, 1995). Nevertheless it was dropped from government priorities after three years, just as its impact was beginning to be felt. Furthermore, the Early Years Study by Athey has never been promoted more widely despite some evidence that its application might even lessen the gap between disadvantaged and other pupils. These interventions have the ability to change pupil outcomes but their potential benefits have not been exploited nor have the limits to their efficacy been properly investigated. In particular, we need to know whether these approaches are especially advantageous with disadvantaged pupils to the extent that they would help close the achievement gap even if used with all pupils.

Although these approaches can clearly combat the individual consequences of disadvantage to some degree, they have so far failed significantly to alter the established differential patterns of achievement in this country. There remains a strong negative correlation between most measures of social disadvantage and school achievement, as even a cursory glance at the league tables of school by school results demonstrates (Smith and Noble, 1995). Why is this so? First, there is the obvious fact that what has been done in compensatory and supplementary activity remains slight in comparison with the impact of the cumulative benefits of growing up in an advantaged home. It would be odd if having warmer, more spacious accommodation, more nutritious food, better health, greater access to books, educational toys and stimulating experiences, and more informed knowledge about how the system works, did not confer considerable advantage in any tests or examinations.

Second, it should not be forgotten that measures of educational achievement are determined by competition within the tradition of a meritocracy. Thus, even though there has been a rise in achievement, as recorded by the General Certificate of Secondary Education results (those gaining the five high grades, usually deemed the mark of success, rose from 22 per cent in 1980 to 44.5 per cent in 1996) more than half the age group still does not succeed at this level (DfEE, 1996a). Given this reality and the factors noted earlier, it would surely be surprising if those with disadvantaged backgrounds succeeded in equal proportions to their more advantaged peers.

Examination success is not, of course, rationed and the official examination boards would be quick to refute any suggestion that they work within strict norms, but it would be naive to think that expectations established over many years could be set aside other than by a slow incremental progression. The annual chorus of more must mean worse ensures that the scope for disadvantaged candidates to join the successful group is likely to remain strictly limited, whatever improvements are made to their absolute levels of achievement.

The Report *Learning Works: Widening Participation in Further Education* (Kennedy, 1997a) has drawn attention to the evidence that it is those who are already well qualified who go on to earn more and to demand and get more learning.

So there remains a need to do a great deal more if an often-declared goal of our education system – to help every child, regardless of family background, achieve up to the limits of his or her potential – is to be realised.

WHAT ELSE CAN BE DONE?

Two possible avenues forward are often seen as mutually exclusive alternatives. One builds on the work in school improvement that has been pioneered as a result of research into school effectiveness. The other is more fundamental and demands change not only to the nature of educational practice but also to the broader social and cultural contexts within which education takes place. We believe that an effective strategy for tackling disadvantage requires movement on both fronts.

3
Change through school improvement

The roots of school improvement lie in 20 years of research into school effectiveness carried out mainly in England, the Netherlands and the United States (Hopkins, Ainscow and West, 1994). The central tenet of school improvement is that the responsibility for change must lie in the hands of the school itself (Stoll and Fink, 1996). In contrast to centrally driven projects, those working in school improvement believe that the head teacher, staff and school governing body – having listened to the views and advice of school inspectors, consultants or researchers – are well placed to decide how best to improve their own institutions (Mortimore, 1996).

Evaluations of established improvement projects show that they tend to have a common pattern (Stoll and Fink, 1996). Initially, the school improvement team carry out an audit of the current state of the school: the pupils' outcomes (including behaviour as well as attainment) the curriculum, the pedagogy, the management of learning, behaviour and resources, and the state of the premises. In the light of such investigations, the team draws up an action plan to enhance the good and repair the bad. Although problems are sometimes obvious, it is often difficult precisely to diagnose their cause. The team has to make a series of hypotheses about what has probably caused which outcome, and what might – if changed – produce a different result. This is far from being an exact science and in the third stage – the evaluation – the team may discover that many outcomes are the result of a complex web of influences and, furthermore, that some changes have produced unintended negative results.

School improvers know they cannot create a recipe book – schools are far too complex for such an approach (Stoll and Myers, 1997; Mortimore, 1998). They have sought, rather, to identify and make use of the underlying processes of change. Writers such as Fullan (1991) Huberman (1992) and Louis and Miles (1990) have identified a number of facilitating or inhibiting factors that affect the process. Fullan, for instance, lists a number of warnings about change that he urges school head teachers to heed: that change is not easy, that conflict and disagreement will be inevitable and that not all colleagues will embrace it. Fullan stresses that heads should expect these outcomes and not be caught unawares if they occur in reaction to change efforts.

Two questions arise from this brief review of improvement strategies: can school improvement help schools that have high proportions of disadvantaged pupils and can it help individual disadvantaged pupils?

CAN IMPROVEMENT PROJECTS HELP SCHOOLS WITH HIGH PROPORTIONS OF DISADVANTAGED PUPILS?

The National Commission on Education (NCE, 1996) undertook a project designed to uncover how some schools with disadvantaged pupils had improved and succeeded against the odds. Eleven teams (each consisting of an educational researcher and two representatives from the business world or the community) carried out fieldwork to identify why particular schools were successful in the face of disadvantage. In the school case study carried out by one of us (Mortimore, Davies and Portway, 1996) we were particularly impressed with the quality of the leadership team and the way it had trusted the majority of the staff to create a set of school aims around the idea of achievement. Pupils were committed to learning and staff held high expectations about examination performance and social behaviour. The confidence of the teachers in the good sense of the pupils – even to the radical point of encouraging them to draw up a code of what they expected of the staff – was impressive.

Maden's and Hillman's (1996) discussion of the findings from all the case studies in the project emphasises the importance of: a leadership stance which builds on and develops a team approach; a vision of success which includes a view of how the school can improve; the careful use of targets; the improvement of the physical environment; common expectations about pupils' behaviour and success; and an investment in good relations with parents and the community. They note how a crisis in the life of the school can become a catalyst for successful change.

What the project demonstrates is that committed and talented heads and teachers can improve schools even if such schools contain a proportion of disadvantaged pupils. In order to achieve improvement, however, such schools have to exceed what could be termed 'normal' efforts. Members of staff have to be more committed and work harder than their peers elsewhere. What is more, they have to maintain the effort so as to sustain the improvement. There can be no switching on the 'automatic pilot' if schools are aiming to buck the trend. We must, however, be aware of the dangers of basing a national strategy for change on the efforts of outstanding individuals working in exceptional circumstances.

A follow-up study compared the school improvement of two London and two Singaporean secondary schools (Mortimore et al., 2000). Interestingly, this study demonstrated that the improvement techniques adopted by heads – motivating staff, focusing on teaching and learning, enhancing the building and changing the school climate – were similar despite the different cultures of the two societies. In Singapore the national attitude towards education was exceptionally positive. The impact of full employment over a period of years and considerably better odds of success in the GCE examinations were also likely to help the motivation of pupils.

Further evidence about the ability of schools with disadvantaged pupils to improve comes from the first tranche of case studies published by the DfEE (1997a). These studies describe some of the ways in which improvement was brought about in schools that had failed their Ofsted inspections. In contrast to much of the rhetoric about resources not mattering, what stands out is the impact of the extra resources invested by the LEAs in their efforts to turn the schools round.

CAN SCHOOL IMPROVEMENT PROJECTS HELP INDIVIDUAL DISADVANTAGED PUPILS?

Evidence from a recent study of the 'value added' results from one local authority shows that some schools are able – once all background factors have been taken into account – to 'lift' the GCSE results by the equivalent of a change from seven grade Ds to seven grade Bs (Thomas and Mortimore, 1996). MacGilchrist (1997) also argues forcefully that some of the special interventions (noted earlier) which have been mounted to support the learning of pupils with special difficulties – and, in many cases, disadvantaged backgrounds – demonstrate that more schools, given adequate support, could help such pupils. She notes, however, that these opportunities have not been sufficiently exploited.

In theory, researchers should be able to estimate fairly precisely how many individual pupils have been helped by their schools to overcome the effects of personal disadvantage. By addressing the GCSE results of secondary schools and noting their intake information from five years before (for example, pupil attainment at the end of primary schooling and how many pupils were eligible for free school meals) it should be possible to estimate some 'value added' scores for their schools in relation to other institutions. Those that had raised the achievement of their 'disadvantaged pupils' significantly beyond what had been achieved by similar pupils in other schools could be assumed to have helped, especially, this group of pupils. The results could then be aggregated to provide an estimate of the likely total number of disadvantaged pupils who have been helped by the efforts of school improvement. Retrospective investigations could then attempt to explore how the schools had helped these pupils and, in particular, whether improvement had been the result of a planned programme or whether it had seemed to occur spontaneously. Other information, such as whether the 'disadvantaged' group had been a particularly high or low proportion of the total, could also be collected so as to inform us about the importance of the educational context in which a pupil learns.

Unfortunately, such an investigation remains a theoretical possibility: not only would it be difficult to ensure that one really was 'comparing like with like', but also there is not a suitable national database which brings together accurate intake and examination outcome data. It is worth noting, anyway, that attributing causal effects to particular initiatives in complex organizations such as schools is always likely to be difficult. Analysis of American statistical evidence suggests that achievement gains are often too readily attributed to a particular initiative when there may well be entirely different explanations, such as a change of intake (Henig, 1994). Without appropriate data and suitably robust analytical techniques, therefore, the evidence for the ability of schools to help individual disadvantaged pupils has to rest on theory and on the historical evidence of those institutions which, in the absence of alternative explanations, do appear to have bucked the trend.

4
Cultural and structural change

Sociologists of education have frequently been critical of work on school effectiveness and school improvement. For example, Angus criticises it for failing 'to explore the relationship of specific practices to wider social and cultural constructions and political and economic interests' (1993: 335). He argues that it 'shifts attention away from the nature of knowledge, the culture of schooling and, most importantly, the question of for whom and in whose interests schools are to be effective' (342). Hatcher (1996) sees school improvement as downplaying the significance of social class, with similar consequences. In this context, even the very term 'disadvantage' can serve to hide the structured inequalities of class and race and actually contribute to the 'colour-blindness' of recent education policy (Gillborn, 1997).

CAN CHANGES IN CURRICULUM AND ASSESSMENT HELP?

Angus's questions suggest that the curriculum itself may be implicated in perpetuating disadvantage by marginalizing the culture of the least powerful groups in society. There is certainly a case for broadening the scope of what counts as legitimate knowledge in schools (Comer, 1980; Whitty, 1985). Some of the National Curriculum Orders have been criticized for adopting an unduly narrow view of worthwhile knowledge and ignoring the pluralism and multi-culturalism of late twentieth-century Britain (Ball, 1993).

Although some of these issues will need to be addressed by the government, individual schools can also play some part in the way they choose to interpret the National Curriculum and they need to be mindful of this opportunity to help the disadvantaged. Trying to counter the cultural bias of current curricular arrangements and making schools more 'inclusive' of diverse communities is sometimes seen as a watering down of standards. Yet schools that are successful with pupils from a variety of backgrounds recognize that high standards can be achieved in a number of ways. While some learning goals need to be tackled by all pupils in the same way, others can be achieved through a variety of routes that take account of different backgrounds. This is not the same as adjusting standards to the lowest common denominator. That is an unacceptable option, especially in the light of the increasing globalization of labour and the need to ensure that young people from the United Kingdom can compete with their peers from elsewhere in the world.

Nevertheless, such considerations also demand that we find ways to ensure that a greater proportion of our pupils can succeed. This may require a restructuring of the assessment system. Can we design a progression system so that a much higher proportion of candidates reaches the currently accepted level of success? The experience of assessing the progress of pupils through the National Curriculum is not very promising and efforts to combine a pupil's need for diagnostic assessment with a system need for certification and monitoring have generally proved unsatisfactory for each of these needs. There are a number of ways in which our national approach to assessment could be improved: the standards set for performance could be better defined; feedback could be more positive; a range of performance tasks and modes could be provided (Gipps, 1994). It has to be borne in mind, however, that such improvements would be more likely to lift overall standards than specifically help the disadvantaged. This would be helpful to our national standards of achievement and is to be greatly encouraged, but clearly does not address the particular problem of the disadvantaged.

It is sometimes suggested that the print-based culture of schools is in itself an obstacle for disadvantaged pupils and that this might be overcome by the new information and communication technologies. It is too early to know whether these will provide dramatic new opportunities. In the past, few schools have had the resources to invest in adequate equipment and too few teachers have been fully trained in its use, though the government has made this one of its priorities. Experiments in particular schools in the United States and in Australia need to be evaluated before we know whether the technology will provide radically more powerful ways of learning. But while it is possible that ICT may help, particularly, pupils from disadvantaged backgrounds, we have to remember that ICTs are shaped by the same social forces as other more obviously social phenomena. For example, any potential benefits for disadvantaged pupils may be offset by the fact that those from advantaged families are more likely to have access to ICT equipment in the home and thus to develop the relevant 'know how' sooner. Furthermore, the Internet, often proclaimed as a democratic medium which eradicates social distinctions, is actually used mainly by white middle-class males and this has consequences for the material available on it (Kenway, 1996). Those developing the National Grid for Learning will need to take these issues into account.

ADDRESSING THE IMPACT OF THE WIDER SOCIETY

Whatever changes occur in the curriculum and means of assessment, it seems inevitable that schools will be affected by their role within a wider society that still maintains social divisions and a powerful sense of hierarchy. A particular criticism of school improvement work is that it has tended to exaggerate the extent to which individual schools can challenge such structural inequalities. Whilst some schools can succeed against the odds, the possibility of them all doing so, year in and year out, still appears remote given that the long-term patterning of educational inequality has been strikingly consistent throughout the history of public education in most countries.

Doubts have recently even been cast on whether Sweden, usually seen as a shining exception, has actually succeeded in bucking this particular trend in recent years (Erikson and Jonsson, 1996). Although there are different theories about how the social and cultural patterning of educational outcomes occurs (Goldthorpe, 1996) these patterns reflect quite closely the relative chances of different groups entering different segments of the labour market. Accordingly, whilst it might be possible, for example, for the ethos of a particular school to help transform the aspirations of a particular group of pupils within it, it seems highly unlikely that all schools could do this in the absence of more substantial social changes.

As noted earlier, one of the depressing findings is that the relative performance of the disadvantaged has remained similar even when the absolute performance of such groups has improved. Just as poverty is a relative concept, we are faced with a situation in which educational success also appears to be partly relative. A large-scale longitudinal study of primary schools carried out by one of us (Mortimore et al., 1988) found that no school reversed the usual 'within school' pattern of advantaged pupils performing better than the disadvantaged. However, some of the disadvantaged pupils in the most effective schools made more progress than their advantaged peers in the least effective schools and even did better in absolute terms. Yet, encouraging as this is, it would appear that, if all primary schools were to improve so that they performed at the level of the most effective, the difference between the overall achievement of the most advantaged social groups and that of the disadvantaged might actually increase.

At secondary level, schools only rarely overcome the relative differences between the performance of different social groups, as the latest evidence on differential school effects demonstrates (Thomas et al., 1997). Moreover, despite the optimism of some school improvement literature, it is still difficult to counter the conclusion to be drawn from a reading of the pioneering *Fifteen Thousand Hours* research (Rutter et al., 1979) that, if all schools performed as well as the best schools, the stratification of achievement by social class would be even more stark than it is now. This would happen because socially advantaged children in highly effective schools would achieve even more than they might do in a less conducive environment and the gap between them and their less advantaged peers would increase.

The initial report of the Literacy Task Force (Literacy Task Force,

1997) seemed to recognize the existence of such problems but underestimated the resource implications of overcoming them. However, New Labour's subsequent literacy strategy, which grew out of the work of that group, does propose a modest redistribution of resources. Nevertheless, the problems and dilemmas facing schools with large numbers of disadvantaged pupils, compared with those with advantaged intakes, are much greater than even current policies recognize (Proudford and Baker, 1995; Thrupp, 1995, 1997). This suggests a continuing need for positive discrimination and the effective targeting of human and material resources. Smith, Smith and Wright (1997) recommend three sets of actions to support schools in disadvantaged areas. They argue that, because of the competitive market that has been created, education in poor areas must not be considered in isolation. Given the existence of this competitive market between schools, they recommend a stronger interventionist role for the LEA. They suggest that 'choice' is too blunt an instrument for improvement and recommend the targeting of resources to schools in disadvantaged areas and possibly a transfer of resources from inspection to school improvement.

Robinson claims that educational measures are unlikely to alleviate the impact of disadvantage. He rightly sees the tackling of social and economic disadvantage as more likely to succeed, arguing that 'a serious programme to alleviate child poverty might do far more for boosting attainment and literacy than any modest intervention in schooling' (Robinson 1997: 17). Unlike Robinson, however, we believe more up-to-date evidence shows that schools can make some difference. Schools with disadvantaged pupils can lift achievement levels, provided those who work in them invest the energy and the dedication to maintain momentum even while working against the grain. Within any school, however, the powerful factors associated with a more advantaged home background appear, in general, to be paramount and this is even more evident when we look across the education system as a whole. It is, therefore, important for government, LEAs and school governors to set challenging goals but it is also important to be clear about the limits of school-based actions. Setting unrealistic goals and adopting a strategy of 'shame and blame' will lead only to cynicism and a lowering of morale amongst those teachers at the heart of the struggle to raise the achievement of disadvantaged pupils.

TACKLING DISADVANTAGE BEYOND THE SCHOOL

Grace has argued that too many urban education reformers have been guilty of 'producing naive school-centred solutions with no sense of the structural, the political and the historical as constraints' (Grace 1984: xii). If schools alone are unable to close the gap between the disadvantaged and their peers, are there other institutions or agencies that can do so? Clearly, if disadvantage has multiple causes, tackling it requires strategies that bring together multiple agencies that more usually work in isolation. There have, of course, been a number of initiatives that have sought to do this in targeted areas (see Wilmott and Hutchinson, 1992) but the recent 'marketization' of housing, health and education appears to have provided disadvantaged families with less rather than more co-ordination of services (Power, Whitty and Youdell, 1995). A major priority for government must surely be to provide incentives for effective multi-agency work to counter disadvantage.

This is not just a matter of ensuring greater efficiency in the delivery of public services, important as that is. Considerable concern has been expressed recently about a decline in 'social capital' in modern societies, with an alleged breakdown in relationships of trust and supportive social networks. Furthermore, there is growing evidence of the damaging effects of vast differences in social capital between different communities (Wilkinson, 1996). Hall (1997: 35) suggests that Britain is becoming increasingly divided between 'a well-connected and active group of citizens and another whose associational life ... is very limited'. Arguably, the situation has been made worse by policies that treat education as a consumer right rather than a citizen right and thereby undermine the notion that education is a public good and the responsibility of the whole community (Whitty, 1997). Yet Coleman's analysis (Coleman, 1988) suggests that the social capital of a community, as well as that of families and schools, can have an important bearing on the educational achievement of its children. Policies that may appear to have little to do with education, such as community development or the building of 'healthy alliances', might therefore actually contribute to the raising of achievement in schools. Thus, statutory agencies could usefully assist voluntary associations in developing networks within the wider community that support the work of schools at the same time as bringing other benefits to the community. The National Healthy Schools Standard, launched by the Department of Health and the Department for Education and Employment, is an example of this and it will be important to evaluate its impact on school effectiveness in disadvantaged areas (Aggleton et al., 2000).

The enhancement of social and cultural capital in disadvantaged areas also requires that more be done to provide opportunities for learning beyond the years of compulsory schooling. Traditionally this has been one of the tasks of further education colleges and adult institutes committed to continuing lifelong learning, but these institutions and their clientele have too often been marginalized within the system as a whole.

The previous government's *Lifetime Learning* (DfEE, 1996b) tried to focus public debate on the importance of lifelong education and training but there are other ways in which, in our view, the government could help disadvantaged people extend their education. These include: a radical revision of its approach to studying whilst unemployed; an extension of tax exemptions for all in post-compulsory training; an equalization of treatment of part-time and full-time students; support for a national credit-based education and training framework; and the provision of increased child care to support learning opportunities for part-time and temporary workers.

The Kennedy Report (1997a) lists a number of detailed recommendations for government, the Training and Enterprise Councils and individual further education colleges. These include: the launching of a lottery-funded government campaign for the creation of a learning nation; the redistribution of public resources towards those with less success in earlier learning; the encouragement of company-funded learning centres for adult workers; and the creation of a unitized system for recognizing achievement (the Pathways to Learning Project).

In a comment on the Report, Kennedy argues (Kennedy, 1997b: 3) that drawing more people into the community of learning is not only central to economic prosperity but also 'one of the most effective ways of tackling social exclusion'. She claims that 'we have been seeing the most terrible separation between rich and poor over the past decades and education has a vital role in redressing the consequences of that division'. This requires 'a redistribution of public resources towards those with less success in earlier learning'. It is not yet clear exactly how far the present government is prepared to move in this direction, even after the proposals in its recent Green and White Papers (DfEE 1998; DfEE 1999; Green and Lucas 1999).

Changes such as those proposed above would ease the financial costs for those who needed to make up in their own time for an unsatisfactory experience of schooling. Such opportunities are necessary if more people are to continue their education and, in particular, if the disadvantaged are to play any part in the formation of a learning society. They are only likely to succeed, however, in the context of a culture – as well as a structure – of inclusiveness. Yet much of our previous history of education has been built on a culture of exclusiveness. It is how to change this culture that probably represents the greatest challenge for government, as has been recognized through the establishment of a Social Exclusion Unit based at the heart of government.

One of the ways to alter this culture is to invent new approaches that bring together partners from across society rather than seeing problems as being solely in the realm of the education service. A commitment to doing this is evident in one of the few New Labour education initiatives that signals a clear break with the policies of the recent past. The government is establishing a programme of Education Action Zones in areas with a mix of underperforming schools and the highest levels of disadvantage (DfEE, 1997b). Such Action Zones will have at their centre a forum of local parents and representatives from local business and community interests in which an action plan and targets will be formulated, implemented and monitored. It remains to be seen how these develop and whether their existence does indeed channel more help and energy into the target areas whilst avoiding the pitfalls of the old Educational Priority Areas. Nevertheless, the idea is worth pursuing, provided each zone's forum includes and values the contribution of all relevant constituencies and provided there really is a significant redistribution of resources into these areas.

5
Conclusions

In this paper we have spelled out our interpretation of the educational problem faced by pupils from disadvantaged families in our society. We have found that – with some notable exceptions – school pupils with such backgrounds do less well than their peers, hardly a surprising finding in a competitive system. We have also shown that previous governments have failed to exploit what knowledge there is about how to combat the problem. In particular, we have described how a number of the co-ordinating initiatives and intervention strategies that appear to have had some success in other countries have been ignored. Furthermore, some of those that have been adopted and shown to have benefits have inexplicably been allowed to wither. Meanwhile, the advantaged have sometimes gained even more than the disadvantaged from those initiatives that have been pursued. The effect is that the advantaged become more so and the disadvantaged – without the help and support of focused extra help – slip further behind. Thus the conventional pattern of outcomes is maintained – with the advantaged at the top and the disadvantaged (with some exceptions) at the bottom. So can there be a solution to this set of problems?

The re-engineering of the educational system, so that dis-advantaged groups can succeed, will not be easy. As Bernstein (1970) noted some 30 years ago, 'Education cannot compensate for society'. Nor is education's role in helping to change society well understood. Probably the single most significant factor that currently distinguishes the most academically successful schools (even if not the most 'effective' ones in value-added terms) is that only a small proportion of their pupils come from disadvantaged homes. To that extent, policies which tackle poverty and related aspects of disadvantage at their roots are likely to be more successful than purely educational interventions in influencing overall patterns of educational inequality. Yet if dynamic school improvement strategies can be developed as one aspect of a broader social policy, then they will have an important role to play on behalf of individual schools and their pupils.

What we have been concerned to stress in this paper is that society needs to be clearer about what schools can and cannot be expected to do. As we have tried to demonstrate, the relationship between individuals, institutions and society is complex and blaming schools for the problems of society is unfair and unproductive. Nevertheless, demonstrating that opportunities for some disadvantaged pupils can be changed in particularly effective schools – even if the disadvantaged as a group still remain behind their peers – can itself help to transform a culture of inertia or despair. It is this transformation that those who work in the field of school improvement are seeking. Schools with high proportions of disadvantaged pupils need extra support. Teachers who choose to work in these schools – because they want to help the disadvantaged – need their commitment recognised and supported rather than being 'blamed', as has happened so shamefully in the past.

In short, we do not consider that there is any single factor that could reverse longstanding patterns of disadvantage but neither do we regard them as an unchangeable fact of life. We believe that our society must – through government actions as well as grass-roots initiatives – begin to adjust the balance between individuals' opportunities and their social responsibilities so as to develop a more equal society. Society should not have to cope with what Wilkinson terms the 'corrosive effects of inequality' (Wilkinson, 1996).

With such a perspective, we consider four clusters of immediate action to be vital:

- better co-ordination of the work of the support agencies by the government and by local authorities;
- early interventions that provide additional educational opportunities for the disadvantaged, funded from an increased education budget;
- reconsideration of the approaches to learning and teaching used with disadvantaged pupils;
- extra support for pupils with disadvantaged backgrounds in school improvement programmes.

Even with these actions we accept that there is unlikely to be a sudden reversal of long-established patterns of disadvantage or any significant long-term change in the absence of concurrent strategies to tackle poverty and disadvantage at their roots. We do consider, however, that the current waste of human resources caused by the educational failure of those with disadvantaged backgrounds is unacceptable in a modern society. We urge the government to make a fresh start. We believe that, if it could focus its energy on this problem and set a new tone by working with local authorities, the teaching and other caring professions, it would have a better chance of achieving change than previous governments. Future generations of school pupils from disadvantaged families would stand to benefit, but the real gain would be the creation of a better educated society more likely to surmount the challenges of the twenty-first century.

References

Acland, H. (1973), 'Social determinants of educational achievement: an evaluation and criticism of research'. Ph.D. Thesis. University of Oxford.

Aggleton, P., Rivers, K., Mulvihill, C., Chase, E., Downie, A., Sinkler, P., Tyrer, P. and Warwick, I. (2000), 'Lessons learned: working towards the National Healthy Schools Standard'. *Health Education*, 100, 3, 102-10.

Alberman, E. D. and Goldstein, H. (1970), 'The "At Risk" Register: a statistical evaluation'. *British Journal of Preventative Medicine*, 24, 3, 129-35.

Angus, L. (1993), 'The Sociology of School Effectiveness'. *British Journal of Sociology of Education*, 14, 3, 333-45.

Athey, C. (1990), *Extending Thought in Young Children*. London: Paul Chapman Publishing.

Ball, S. J. (1993), 'Education, Majorism and "the Curriculum of the Dead"', *Curriculum Studies*, 1, 2, 195-214.

Bandura, A. (1995), 'Exercise of personal and collective efficacy in changing societies'. In A. Bandura (ed.), *Self Efficacy in Changing Societies*. Cambridge: Cambridge University Press.

Bernstein, B. (1970), 'Education cannot compensate for society'. *New Society*, 387, 344-7.

Brannen, J., Moss, P., Owen, C. and Wale, C. (1997), *Mothers, Fathers and Employment: Parents and the labour market in Britain 1984-1994*. London: DfEE/Institute of Education.

Brown, P., Halsey, A. H., Lauder, H. and Wells, A. (1997), 'The Transformation of Education and Society: An introduction', In A.H. Halsey, H. Lauder, P. Brown and A. Wells (eds), *Education: Culture, economy and society*. Oxford: Oxford University Press.

Clay, M. M. (1982), *Observing Young Readers*. New Hampshire: Heinemann.

Coleman, J. (1988), 'Social capital in the creation of human capital'. *American Journal of Sociology*, 94, Supplement, 95-120.

Comer, J. P. (1980), *School Power: Implication of an intervention project*. New York: Free Press.

Davie, R., Butler, N. and Goldstein, H. (1972), *From Birth to Seven*. Harlow: Longman.

Dennehy, A., Smith, L. and Harker, P. (1997), 'Not to be ignored: young people, poverty and health'. In A. Walker and C. Walker (eds) *Britain Divided: The growth of social exclusion in the 1980s and 1990s*. London: CPAG.

DfEE (Department for Education and Employment) (1996a), *Education Statistics*. London: HMSO.

— (1996b), *Lifetime Learning: A policy framework*. London: DfEE.

— (1997a), *The Road to Success*. London: Institute of Education/DfEE.

— (1997b), *Excellence in Schools*. London: Stationery Office.

— (1998), *The Learning Age: A renaissance for a new Britain*. London: Stationery Office.

— (1999), *Learning to Succeed: A new framework for post-16 learning.* London: Stationery Office.

Douglas, J. W. B. (1964), *The Home and the School.* London: MacGibbon & Kee.

Edwards, T., Fitz, J. and Whitty, G. (1989), *The State and Private Education: An evaluation of the Assisted Places Scheme.* Lewes: Falmer Press.

Erikson, R. and Jonsson, J. O. (eds) (1996), *Can Education be Equalized? The Swedish Case in Comparative Perspective.* Boulder, CO: Westview Press.

Essen, J. and Wedge, P. (1982), *Continuities in Childhood Disadvantage.* London: Heinemann.

Eurostat (1997), Reported in the *Guardian,* 28 April.

Fullan, M. (1991), *The New Meaning of Educational Change.* London: Cassell.

Gillborn, D. (1997), 'Young, black and failed by school: the market, education reform and black students'. *Journal of Inclusive Education,* 1, 1, 65-87.

Gipps, C. (1994), *Beyond Testing: Towards a theory of educational assessment.* London: Falmer Press.

Goldthorpe, J. H. (1996), 'Class analysis and the reorientation of class theory: the case of persisting differentials in educational attainment'. *British Journal of Sociology,* 47, 3, 482-505.

Gorman, T. and Fernandes, C. (1992), *Reading in Recession.* Slough: NFER.

Grace, G. (1984), *Education in the City.* London: Routledge & Kegan Paul.

Green, A. and Lucas, N. (eds) (1999), *FE and Lifelong Learning: Realigning the sector for the twenty-first century.* London: Institute of Education.

Hall, P. A. (1997), 'Social capital: a fragile asset'. In I. Christie and H. Perry (eds), *The Wealth and Poverty of Networks: Tackling social exclusion.* London: Demos.

Halsey, A. H. (ed.) (1972), *Educational Priority, E.P.A. Problems and Policies, I.* London: HMSO.

Hatcher, R. (1996), 'The limitations of the new social democratic agendas'. In R. Hatcher and K. Jones (eds), *Education after the Conservatives*. Stoke-on-Trent: Trentham Books.

Henig, J. R. (1994), *Rethinking School Choice: Limits of the market metaphor*. Princeton: Princeton University Press.

Herman, R. and Stringfield, S. (1995), *Ten Promising Programmes for Educating Disadvantaged Students*. Baltimore: Johns Hopkins University.

Hobsbaum, A. (1995), Reading recovery in England'. *Literacy, Teaching and Learning*, 1, 2, 21-39.

Holtermann, S. (1997), 'All our futures: the impact of public expenditure and fiscal policies on children and young people'. In A. Walker and C. Walker (eds), *Britain Divided: The growth of social exclusion in the 1980s and 1990s*. London: CPAG.

Hopkins, D., Ainscow, M. and West, M. (1994), *School Improvement in an Era of Change*. London: Cassell.

Huberman, M. (1992), Critical introduction to Fullan, M., *Successful School Improvement*. Buckingham: Open University Press.

Kennedy, H. (1997a), *Learning Works: Widening participation in Further Education*, London: FEFC.

— (1997b), 'The Report'. *Guardian Education*, July 1, 2-3.

Kenway, J. (1996a), 'The information superhighway and post-modernity: the social promise and the social price'. *Comparative Education*. 32, 2, 217-31.

Literacy Task Force (1997), *A Reading Revolution: How we can teach every child to read well*. London: Literacy Task Force.

Louis, K. and Miles, M. (1990), *Improving the Urban High School*. New York: Teachers College Press.

MacBeath, J. and Turner, M. (1990), *Learning out of School: Homework, policy and practice*. A research study commissioned by the Scottish Education Department. Glasgow: Jordanhill College.

MacGilchrist, B. (1997), 'Reading and achievement'. *Research Papers in Education*, 12, 2, 157-76.

Maden, M. and Hillman, J. (1996), 'Lessons in success'. In National Commission on Education, *Success Against the Odds*. London: Routledge.

Mortimore, J. and Blackstone, T. (1982), *Education and Disadvantage*. London: Heinemann.

Mortimore, P. (1996), 'Partnership and co-operation in school improvement'. Paper presented at the Association for Teacher Education in Europe Conference, Glasgow, Scotland, September.

— (1998), *The Road to Improvement*. Lisse: Swets and Zeitlinger.

Mortimore, P. and Mortimore, J. (1986), 'Education and social class'. In R. Rogers (ed.), *Education and Social Class*. Lewes: Falmer.

Mortimore, P., Sammons, P., Stoll, L., Lewis, D. and Ecob, R. (1988), 'The effects of school membership on pupils' educational outcomes'. *Research Papers in Education*, 3, 1, 3-26.

Mortimore, P., Davies, H. and Portway, S. (1996), 'Burntwood School: a case study'. In NCE, *Success Against the Odds*. London: Routledge.

Mortimore, P., Gopinathan, S., Leo, E., Myers, K., Sharpe, L., Stoll, L. and Mortimore, J. (2000), *The Culture of Change: Case studies of improving schools in Singapore and London*. London: Institute of Education.

NCE (National Commission on Education) (1996), *Success Against the Odds: Effective schools in disadvantaged areas*. London: Routledge.

Nunes, T., Schliemann, A. D. and Carraher, D. W. (1993), *Street Mathematics and School Mathematics*. Cambridge: Cambridge University Press.

OECD (1995), *Our Children at Risk*. Paris: OECD.

Oppenheim, C. (1993), *Poverty: the facts*. London: CPAG.

Osborne, A. F. and Milbank, J. E. (1987), *The Effects of Early Education*. Oxford: Clarendon Press.

Plewis, I. (1997), Letter to the *Times Educational Supplement*, 9 May.

Power, S., Whitty, G. and Youdell, D. (1995), *No Place to Learn: Homelessness and education*. London: Shelter.

Proudford, C. and Baker, R. (1995), 'Schools that make a difference: a sociological perspective on effective schooling'. *British Journal of Sociology of Education*, 16, 3, 277-292.

Robinson, P. (1997). *Literacy, Numeracy and Economic Performance*. London: CEP/London School of Economics.

Rowe, K. J. (1995), 'Factors affecting students' progress in reading: key findings from a longitudinal study in literacy', *Teaching and Learning, an International Journal of Early Literacy*, 1, 2, 57-110.

Rutter, M., Maughan, B., Mortimore, P. and Ouston, J. (1979), *Fifteen Thousand Hours*. London: Paul Chapman Publishing.

Sammons, P., Kysel, F. and Mortimore, P. (1983), 'Educational priority indices: a new perspective', *British Educational Research Journal*, 9, 1, 27-40.

Schweinhart, L. J. and Weikart, D. P. (1997), 'Lasting differences: the High/Scope Pre-School curriculum comparison study through age 23'. *Early Childhood Research Quarterly*, 12, 117-43.

Slavin, R. E., Karweit, N. L., Dolan, L. J., Wasik, B. A. and Madden, N. A. (1993), '"Success for all": longitudinal effects of a restructuring program for inner city elementary schools'. *American Educational Research Journal*, 30, 123-48.

Smith, G. (1987), 'Whatever happened to educational priority areas?' *Oxford Review of Education*, 13, 1.

Smith, G., Smith, T. and Wright, G. (1997), 'Poverty and schooling: choice, diversity or division?' In A. Walker and C. Walker (eds), *Britain Divided: The growth of social exclusion in the 1980s and 1990s*. London: CPAG.

Smith, T. and Noble, M. (1995), *Education Divides: Poverty and schooling in the 1990s*. London: CPAG.

Stoll, L. and Fink, D. (1996), *Changing our Schools*. Buckingham: Open University Press.

Stoll, L. and Myers, K. (1997), *No Quick Fixes: Perspectives on schools in difficulty*. London: Falmer Press.

Sylva, K. and Hurry, J. (1995), 'The effectiveness of reading recovery and phonological training for children with reading problems'. Full Report prepared for the School Curriculum and Assessment Authority. London: Thomas Coram Research Unit, University of London, Institute of Education.

Thomas, S. and Mortimore, P. (1996), 'Comparison of value added models for secondary school effectiveness'. *Research Papers in Education.* 11, 1, 5-33.

Thomas, S., Sammons, P., Mortimore, P. and Smees, R. (1997), 'Stability and consistency in secondary schools' effect on students' GCSE outcomes over 3 years'. *School Effectiveness and School Improvement,* 9, 2, 169-97.

Thrupp, M. (1995), 'The school mix effect: the history of an enduring problem in educational research, policy and practice'. *British Journal of Sociology of Education,* 16, 183-203.

— (1997), 'The art of the possible: organising and managing high and low socio-economic schools'. Paper presented to the annual meeting of the American Educational Research Association, Chicago, March 24-8.

Tizard, J., Schofield, W. and Hewison, J. (1982), 'Symposium: reading-collaboration between teachers and parents in assisting children's reading'. *British Journal of Educational Psychology,* 52, 1, 1-15.

Townsend, P. (1996), Comment quoted in Richards, H., 'Perspectives'. *Times Higher Educational Supplement,* 30 August, 13.

Walker, A. and Walker, C. (eds.) (1997), *Britain Divided: The growth of social exclusion in the 1980s and 1990s.* London: CPAG.

Weikart, D. P. (1972), 'Relationship of curriculum, teaching and learning in pre-school education'. In J. C. Stanley (ed.) *Preschool Programs for the Disadvantaged.* Baltimore: Johns Hopkins University Press.

Whitty, G. (1985), *Sociology and School Knowledge.* London: Methuen.

— (1997), 'School autonomy and parental choice: consumer rights versus citizen rights in education policy in Britain'. In D. Bridges (ed.) *Education, Autonomy and Democratic Citizenship in a Changing World.* London: Routledge.

Whitty, G., Power, S. and Halpin, D. (1998), *Devolution and Choice in Education: The school, the state and the market.* Buckingham; Open University Press.

Wilkinson, R. (1996), *Unhealthy Societies: The afflictions of inequality.* London: Routledge.

— (1997), *Unfair Shares: The effects of widening income differences on the welfare of the young.* London: Barnardos.

Wilmott, P. and Hutchinson, R. (1992), *Urban Trends 1.* London: Policy Studies Institute.